You First!

Kids Talk About Consideration

Written by Pamela Hill Nettleton ••• Illustrated by Amy Bailey Muehlenhardt

Thanks to our advisers for their expertise, research, and advice:

Stephanie Goerger Sandahl, M.A., Counseling
Lutheran Social Services of Minnesota
Fergus Falls, Minnesota

Susan Kesselring, M.A., Literacy Educator
Rosemount-Apple Valley-Eagan (Minnesota) School District

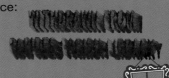

PICTURE WINDOW BOOKS
Minneapolis, Minnesota

Managing Editors: Bob Temple, Catherine Neitge
Creative Director: Terri Foley
Editors: Brenda Haugen, Christianne Jones
Editorial Adviser: Andrea Cascardi
Designer: Nathan Gassman
Page production: Picture Window Books
The illustrations in this book were rendered digitally.

Picture Window Books
5115 Excelsior Boulevard
Suite 232
Minneapolis, MN 55416
877-845-8392
www.picturewindowbooks.com

Printed in the United States of America.

Library of Congress Cataloging-in-Publication Data
Nettleton, Pamela Hill.
You first! : kids talk about consideration / written by Pamela Hill Nettleton ;
    illustrated by Amy Bailey Muehlenhardt.
p. cm. — (Kids talk)
Includes bibliographical references and index.
ISBN 1-4048-0624-5 (reinforced library binding : alk. paper)
1.Thoughtfulness—Miscellanea—Juvenile literature. I. Muehlenhardt,
    Amy Bailey, 1974- II. Title. III. Series.

BJ1533.T45N48 2004
177'.7—dc22
                                                        2003028234

To my children, Gretchen,
Christopher, and Ian,
who give the best advice

Dear Kyle,

Whoever had your book last year kept it neat for you, right? What if someone had spilled orange juice in your math book? The pages would be stuck together. Your homework would be all messed up from missing the problems printed on the juicy pages. Yuck!

Your teacher is showing you how to be considerate. It may seem stupid at first, but give it a try! Hey—you could even use really cool paper to cover your book. Then you can make your boring textbook look cool!

Tina

Hi! My name is Tina Truly, and this is my advice column. Kids like you write me letters about tough stuff, and I kick in a little friendly advice. Now that I'm 13, I have a ton of advice to give!

I'll bet you give lots and lots of advice to your friends. You tell them how to play ball better, if their clothes look cool, and which movies to go see, right? Well, that's kind of what I do here. I tell you what I think.

Today's topic is consideration. Being considerate means thinking of other people's feelings. Since I live with my big brother, Josh, that's something I have a lot of practice doing!

My dad, my stepmom, and my mom help me remember to be considerate when I forget. Now I'm passing my wisdom on to you!

Sincerely,

Tina Truly

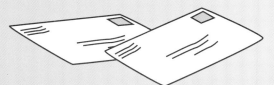

Dear Tina,

My teacher, Miss Rand, says we have to take care of our textbooks. We can't draw on the pages. We have to put paper on each book so the covers don't get dirty. What's the big deal? They're just old textbooks. Who cares if they get worn out or messed up?

Kylie

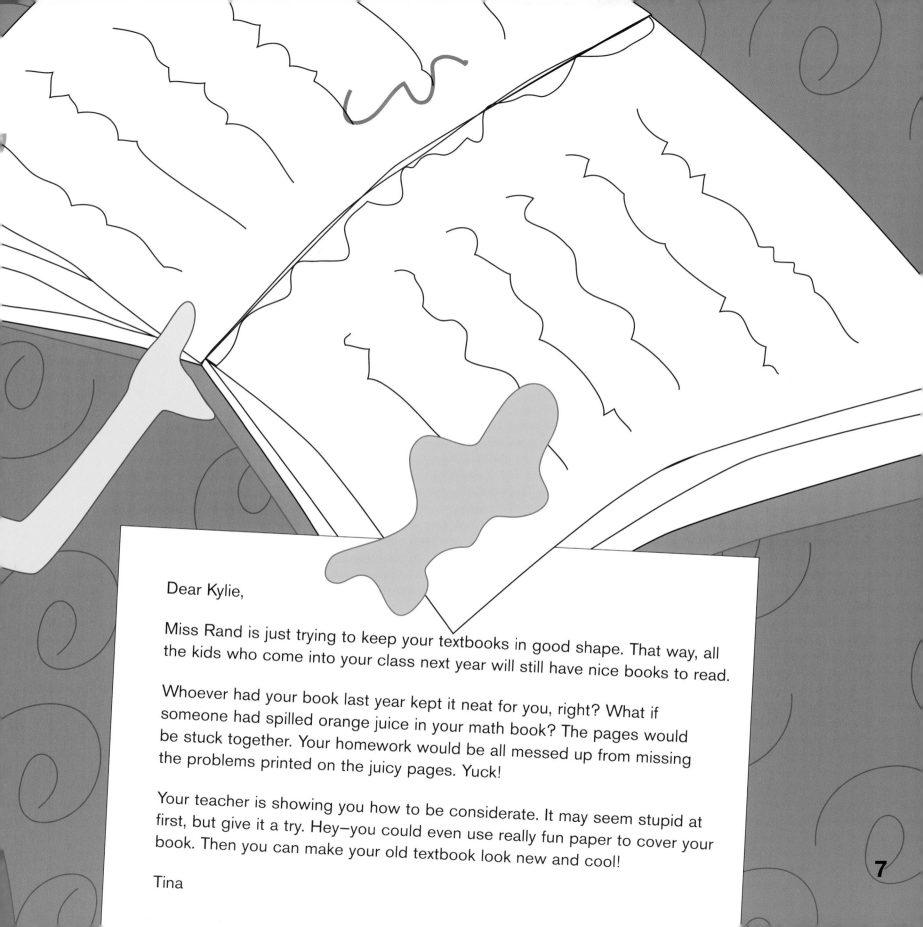

Dear Kylie,

Miss Rand is just trying to keep your textbooks in good shape. That way, all the kids who come into your class next year will still have nice books to read.

Whoever had your book last year kept it neat for you, right? What if someone had spilled orange juice in your math book? The pages would be stuck together. Your homework would be all messed up from missing the problems printed on the juicy pages. Yuck!

Your teacher is showing you how to be considerate. It may seem stupid at first, but give it a try. Hey—you could even use really fun paper to cover your book. Then you can make your old textbook look new and cool!

Tina

Dear Tina,

There are so many goofy rules in our school. Be quiet in the halls. Walk—don't run. Stay on the right side of the hall. I think the principal just thinks up silly rules all day so she can tell us what to do. Do you have rules at your school?

A.J.

Dear A.J.,

I'm in seventh grade at Meandering Middle School, and you'd better believe we have rules! I agree with you—some rules seem pretty silly. The rules you're talking about make sense, though.

Did you ever sit in a classroom and hear laughing, yelling, and noise in the hall? You wonder what's going on out there. You wonder if the person laughing is your friend. When the noise dies down and you start to listen to your teacher again, you missed a really important part of your math lesson. Bummer!

If you run in the halls, you could fall on your nose. That's a good thing to avoid. How embarrassing! You could even knock someone else over, which is also embarrassing.

The staying-on-the-right-side-of-the-hall thing is a really good idea, too. Between classes here at Meandering Middle School, the halls are jammed. If we didn't stay to the right, no one would move, and everyone would be wedged in the hall all day.

You may not love the rules, but be considerate of them.

Tina

Dear Tina,

Why can't I drink right out of the milk carton and then put it back in the refrigerator? My sister, Katie, says it's gross.

Patrick

Dear Patrick,

Yuck! It is gross! I don't want to drink out of any milk carton that you've been sucking on, no matter how nice of a kid you are. It's a good way to share germs and catch a cold, too.

You need to be considerate of other people, Patrick. You aren't the only one who lives in your house. Pour your milk into a glass, please. Don't forget to put the carton back in the fridge, and don't even think about putting it back if it's empty!

Tina

Thank

Dear Tina,

My grandma lives far away. She sent me a new video game for my birthday. My mom says I should write her a thank-you note. What am I supposed to say in it?

Robby

Dear Robby,

Sounds like you have a cool grandma! Mine sends me socks and underwear. Definitely not as fun as a video game!

When someone passes you the macaroni and cheese at dinner, you say "thank you," don't you? A thank-you note is just another way of saying "thank you."

My stepmom says that writing a thank-you note is a little way of sending the love back. Your grandma probably imagined how excited you'd be when you opened your new video game. Since she lives far away, she couldn't be there to watch you open the gift. A thank-you note helps show her how her gift made you feel. That will mean a lot to her.

Now, how to write that thank-you note. Sit down with a piece of paper and a pencil. You can even fold the paper like a card. Pretend your grandma is sitting right across the table from you. You don't have to get all fancy. Just tell her how you feel. Something like, "Hi, Grandma! It was so cool that you remembered my birthday. The video game is totally awesome! How did you know I wanted that one? I've already played it five times. I love you, Grandma. Thanks for the great birthday present. Love, Robby."

She'll love to hear from you!

Tina

Dear Tina,

I read a story about a girl who liked to do what she called random acts of kindness. She would do nice things for people for no special reason. My mom says that would be a considerate thing for me to do now and then. Do you have any good ideas of kind things to do for people?

Mona

Dear Mona,

What an awesome idea! I think it is so cool that you are going to try to do this. There are so many things you can do!

Here are some ideas to get you started:

At home, you can shovel the driveway for your dad. If your mom says she's hungry, you can make her a sandwich. You can carry your big brother's backpack upstairs to his bedroom for him.

At school, you can say, "Hello," to the new kid. You can smile at your teacher. You can give your friend a special treat at lunch for getting an A on the big test.

When my friend Keesha broke her leg, my dad helped me bake her cookies. My stepmom drove me over to Keesha's house to deliver them.

You will have even better ideas because you know your own family and friends. You'll be able to think of really great stuff to do!

Tina

Dear Tina,

My mom says I should hold the door open for my aunt. She also tells me to help my grandmother in and out of the car. I'm happy to do these things, but I was wondering why girls don't have to do these things for boys?

Amal

Dear Amal,

What a good question!

It doesn't matter if you are a boy or a girl, holding a door open is a considerate thing to do. I think this rule originally came from a time when doors were big and heavy, and it was the custom for men to hold them open for women and children. Now, it's just polite to hold the door open for the next person.

It is really cool for a kid to hold a door open for an older person because it shows respect. It's also considerate to help older people in and out of the car. It's a lot harder for them to get in and out, and it's nice if you can lend a helping hand. Plus, it's always nice to help your grandma or grandpa.

Tina

Dear Tina,

When there is only one piece of pizza left, my mom says I need to ask my friends if they want it before I just take it. What's up with that?

Maggie

Dear Maggie,

Hmmm. A great piece of pizza is hard to give up, isn't it? Your mom is just teaching you to think about your friends' feelings first. She is teaching you how to be considerate.

If there are three friends and only one piece of pizza left, someone has to share. It's considerate of you to ask your two friends if they would like the piece. You could also ask if they'd like to split it with you, and cut it into three pieces. No matter how delicious that pepperoni looks, grabbing the last slice and stuffing it into your mouth is just rude.

So ask, "Who'd like this last piece of pizza?" and pass the box around. It's a way of being a good friend and being considerate.

Tina

22

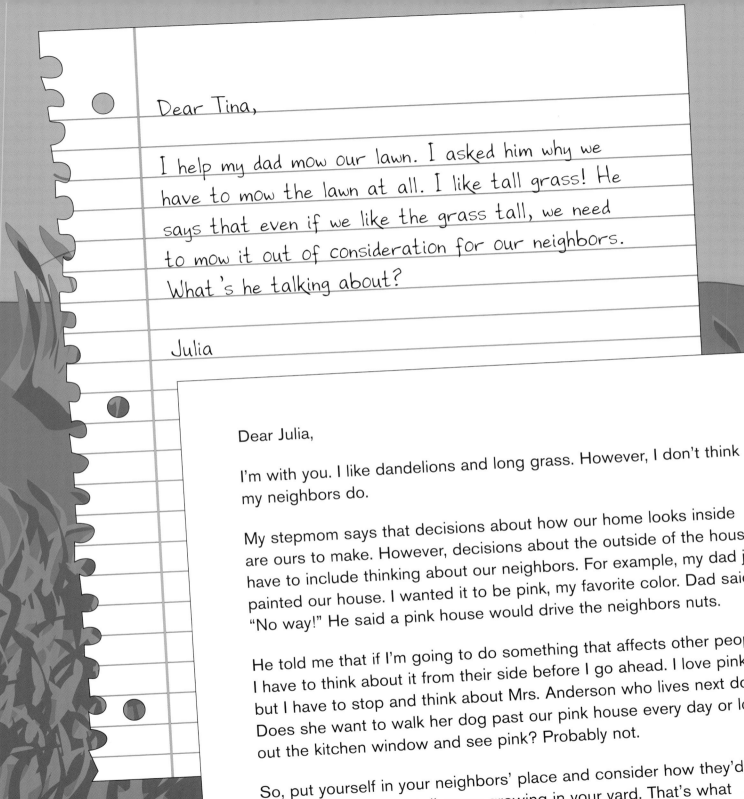

Dear Tina,

I help my dad mow our lawn. I asked him why we have to mow the lawn at all. I like tall grass! He says that even if we like the grass tall, we need to mow it out of consideration for our neighbors. What's he talking about?

Julia

Dear Julia,

I'm with you. I like dandelions and long grass. However, I don't think my neighbors do.

My stepmom says that decisions about how our home looks inside are ours to make. However, decisions about the outside of the house have to include thinking about our neighbors. For example, my dad just painted our house. I wanted it to be pink, my favorite color. Dad said, "No way!" He said a pink house would drive the neighbors nuts.

He told me that if I'm going to do something that affects other people, I have to think about it from their side before I go ahead. I love pink, but I have to stop and think about Mrs. Anderson who lives next door. Does she want to walk her dog past our pink house every day or look out the kitchen window and see pink? Probably not.

So, put yourself in your neighbors' place and consider how they'd feel about looking at tall grass growing in your yard. That's what consideration is all about.

Tina

23

Dear Tina,

My friend Cissy and I love to try on clothes at the store, but Cissy takes so long! She hangs each dress back up. She folds each sweater just like it was before she tried it on. I tell her to just leave the clothes in a heap on the floor. Picking them up is the job of the store clerks. What can I do to speed Cissy up?

24

Amanda

Dear Amanda,

Whoa, girl! Don't try to speed Cissy up. Instead, I hope Cissy's awesome manners rub off on you!

Do you want to walk into a dressing room that has someone else's mess all over the floor? I'll bet your answer is "no way!" Don't leave that mess behind for the next kids who walk through the door. They'll think you're a major slob. The clerks won't be happy to see you come back again, either.

Polite people pick up after themselves. Bend over, and pick up those cute pants yourself, Amanda. You'll get to be considerate and get some pretty good exercise, too!

Tina

Dear Tina,

My stepbrother chews with his mouth open. When I have to watch him eat and see the food fall out of his mouth, it makes me sick. You try it!

Nicole

Now I'll be considerate to you and say thank you for all your great letters. Hey, we're not done yet! Turn the page!

Dear Nicole,

No thanks! Just thinking about it makes me gag. Yuck!

One day at dinner, my brother, Josh, said he thought the whole point of table manners was to not gross out anyone else at the table. My stepmom laughed, but she said he was right. "Don't gross out the people you're with" is a pretty good rule to eat by. It sounds like it's a rule your stepbrother needs to hear.

You could just yell at him from across the table, "Hey, dude! I don't want to watch you chew your peanut butter sandwich! Shut your mouth!" However, this might get you grounded you for a week. A better idea might be to tell him when it's just the two of you, so he doesn't feel stupid. Try something simple like, "Hey, Tommy, can you please close your mouth while you chew?"

The thing is, your stepbrother needs to learn some table manners at home so he doesn't embarrass himself in public. One day at school, some kid is going to tease him about it, and he'll feel awful. You're doing your stepbrother a favor by helping him out now.

Tina

It's Quiz Time

Yes, it's a quiz. No worries, though, this is a fun one! Grab a piece of paper and a pencil, and get started.

1. You should cover your textbooks with:
   - A. a blanket.
   - B. gum.
   - C. paper.

2. The rules in school were made up by:
   - A. elves.
   - B. mad scientists.
   - C. grown-ups who want you to be safe.

3. A random act of kindness is:
   - A. doing something good for someone else just to be nice.
   - B. a really goofy thing to do.
   - C. often painful.

4. In a thank-you note, you should say:
   - A. I didn't like the gift you gave me.
   - B. my mom said I had to write this stupid thank-you note.
   - C. it was nice of you to remember me.

5. When you're walking into a store, hold the door open for:
   - A. the person behind you.
   - B. a bat that's trying to fly in.
   - C. as many mosquitoes as possible.

6. If you take the last piece of pizza:
   - A. your friends will think you are cool.
   - B. your friends might be mad you didn't share.
   - C. you'll burp.

7. Your neighbors will love you if you:
   - A. use their garden for third base in baseball.
   - B. help keep your yard looking nice.
   - C. paint "Hi, neighbor!" on the side of your house.

8. When you leave a mess behind you in a store:
   - A. the clerks will love to clean up after you.
   - B. you'll get to be on TV.
   - C. you are not being considerate.

9. You have good table manners if:
   - A. food falls out of your mouth when you talk.
   - B. your friends refuse to sit with you while you eat.
   - C. you chew with your mouth closed.

10. If you drink right out of the milk carton, you should:
    - A. stop it! Be polite and grab a glass.
    - B. also eat jam right out of the jar.
    - C. suck eggs right out of their shells.

Answer Key: 1-C, 2-C, 3-A, 4-C, 5-A, 6-B, 7-B, 8-C, 9-C, 10-A

Using good manners is one way to be considerate. A great role model for consideration is Emily Post. Emily was one of the first people to write down lots of the rules about how to eat, how to answer the door, how to write thank-you letters, and other cool stuff.

Emily's book of etiquette became a big hit. Through the years, Emily rewrote the book to keep up with the times. For example, her first book on etiquette was written in 1922 and has rules about how your butler should answer the door. Not a big worry these days!

Emily was born in Maryland and lived from 1873 to 1960. She had a newspaper column and a radio show about good manners. Emily said manners are not silly. Manners, she said, are about being honest, kind, and respectful.

Emily wrote funny books and stories, too, but she is most famous for her books on etiquette. Emily's children and grandchildren keep writing down the rules of etiquette as times change. There are even rules now for how to write on the Internet!

Words to Know

Here are some of my favorite words and expressions from today's letters.

advice–suggestions from people who think they know what you should do about a problem

clerk–a person who works at a store and helps you pick out cool stuff

etiquette–the rules for acting in a polite way; for instance, it's not good etiquette to put your stinky feet on the table when people are eating–or at any time, for that matter

random–for no special reason; if something happens in a random way, it happens now and then, but you can't guess when

wisdom–the stuff you learn as you get older

To Learn More

At the Library

Eberly, Sheryl. *365 Manners Kids Should Know: Games, Activities, and Other Fun Ways to Help Children Learn Etiquette.* New York: Three Rivers Press, 2001.

Suben, Eric. *Manners.* Vero Beach, Florida: Rourke Book Co., 1999.

Weber, Rebecca. *Understanding Differences.* Minneapolis: Compass Point Books, 2004.

On the Web

FactHound offers a safe, fun way to find Web sites related to this book. All of the sites on FactHound have been researched by our staff. *www.facthound.com*

1. Visit the FactHound home page
2. Enter a search word related to this book, or type in this special code: 1404806245.
3. Click on the FETCH IT button.

Your trusty FactHound will fetch the best Web sites for you!

Index

Books in This Series

- **Do I Have To? Kids Talk About Responsibility**
- **How Could You? Kids Talk About Trust**
- **I Can Do It! Kids Talk About Courage**
- **Is That True? Kids Talk About Honesty**
- **Let's Get Along! Kids Talk About Tolerance**
- **May I Help You? Kids Talk About Caring**
- **No Fair! Kids Talk About Fairness**
- **Pitch In! Kids Talk About Cooperation**
- **Treat Me Right! Kids Talk About Respect**
- **Want to Play? Kids Talk About Friendliness**
- **We Live Here Too! Kids Talk About Good Citizenship**
- **You First! Kids Talk About Consideration**